INSTRUCTIONS

FOR

AMERICAN SERVICEMEN

IN

IRAQ DURING
WORLD WAR II

PAGES 1–44 OF THIS BOOK ARE A
FACSIMILE OF A "POCKET GUIDE" PREPARED BY
THE SPECIAL SERVICE DIVISION OF THE ARMY SERVICE
FORCES, UNITED STATES ARMY IN 1943.

. . . .

ALL SPELLINGS AND PUNCTUATION
ARE REPRODUCED AS THEY APPEAR
IN THE ORIGINAL 1943
PUBLICATION.

INSTRUCTIONS

FOR

AMERICAN SERVICEMEN

IN

IRAQ DURING
WORLD WAR II

WITH A NEW FOREWORD BY
LIEUTENANT COLONEL JOHN A. NAGL

THE UNIVERSITY OF CHICAGO PRESS ★ CHICAGO AND LONDON

Pages 1–44 of this book are a facsimile of a "pocket guide" prepared by the Special Service Division of the Army Service Forces, United States Army in 1943.

This work is reproduced with the kind assistance of the Special Collections Research Center at Regenstein Library, the University of Chicago.

The University of Chicago Press, Chicago 60637
The University of Chicago Press, Ltd., London

Foreword by John A. Nagl
© 2007 by The University of Chicago
All rights reserved. Published 2007

Printed in the United States of America

12 11 10 09 08 07   1 2 3 4 5 6

ISBN-13: 978-0-226-84170-0 (cloth)
ISBN-10: 0-226-84170-7 (cloth)

Library of Congress
Cataloging-in-Publication Data

United States. Army Service Forces. Special Service Division.
Instructions for American servicemen in Iraq during World War II / [Special Service Division of the Army Service Forces] ; with a new foreword by LTC John A. Nagl.
    p. cm.
"Pages 1–44 of this book are a facsimile of a 'pocket guide' prepared by the Special Service Division of the Army Service Forces, United States Army in 1943."
ISBN-13: 978-0-226-84170-0 (cloth : alk. paper)
ISBN-10: 0-226-84170-7 (cloth : alk. paper)
1. Iraq. 2. National characteristics, Iraqi. I. Nagl, John A., 1966– II. Title.
DS79.U6   2007
956.7—dc22

                                    2007006100

♾ The paper used in this publication meets the minimum requirements of the American National Standard for Information Sciences—Permanence of Paper for Printed Library Materials, ANSI Z39.48-1992.

A SHORT GUIDE TO
"A SHORT GUIDE TO IRAQ"

(1943)

History doesn't repeat itself, but it often rhymes. This wonderful guide was prepared to inform American troops assigned to Iraq in 1943 how best to assist the British guarding it against Nazi infiltration.[1] It would be just as useful to those assigned there today; indeed, I wish that I had read it before beginning my own yearlong tour in Al Anbar in late 2003!

Some of the guidance in this little book is eerie to anyone who has fought in Iraq recently: "That tall man in the flowing robe you are going to see soon, with the whiskers and the long hair, is a first-class fighting man, highly skilled in guerrilla warfare. Few fighters in any country, in fact, excel him in that kind of situation. If he is your friend, he can be a staunch and

1. Iraq has always been a complicated place. In May of 1941 the British were forced to reimpose a friendly government after a pro-Nazi insurgency had temporarily deposed their man in Iraq the previous month.

valuable ally. If he should happen to be your enemy—watch out!" Would that we had listened to the warning that the Arabs are skilled guerilla fighters, a warning trumpeted exactly sixty years later by retired Marine Colonel Gary Anderson in April of 2003, even before Baghdad had fallen.

Would also that we had listened to lessons already learned but long forgotten, advice such as "The nomads are divided into tribes headed by sheikhs. These leaders are very powerful and should be shown great consideration." A policy that showed greater consideration to the Sunni sheiks and to their interests in the immediate aftermath of the toppling of Saddam Hussein's regime in 2003 might have prevented the fervent insurgency from being raised to the fever pitch it has taken recently—for, as the 1943 guide warns in stunning understatement, "The Iraqis have some religious and tribal differences among themselves."

It is almost impossible, when reading this guide, not to slap oneself on the forehead in despair that the Army knew so much of Arabic culture and customs, and of the importance of that knowledge for achieving military success in Iraq, six decades ago—and forgot almost all of those lessons in the intervening years. It is a sad fact of history that armies all but invariably forget the lessons of prior campaigns and have to relearn them from scratch when war begins again, at the cost of too many soldiers' and civilian lives. One hopes that the re-publication of this little field guide will help the Army remember how much it has learned while fighting today's campaigns against insurgencies in Iraq and Afghanistan, and vow not to have to pay for these lessons in blood yet again.

The guide is particularly good on religious customs and courtesies that bedeviled my unit, the 1st Brigade of the 1st Infantry Division. As the month of fasting called Ramadan approached in November 2003, I would have appreciated knowing that "Moslem tempers are very short during this month as yours would be under similar circumstances"—and perhaps I would have been better prepared for the surge of violence that marked this celebration in our sector. Guerrilla fighters are particularly willing to sacrifice their lives in Ramadan as a result of the benefits promised to them in the afterlife if they fall during the festival, and many of them made that choice in Al Anbar during Ramadan in 2003.

The single topic on which the field guide focuses most time and attention is the very issue with which I struggled most vigorously and unsuccessfully back in 2004: the Arabic language. It is impossible to build personal relationships with local leaders, police chiefs, and Iraqi army officers without being able to engage in dialogue with them, but capable, trustworthy interpreters were my scarcest resource. Interpreters are the public face of the counterinsurgency effort to the local population; on their words hinges success or failure. I managed them as carefully as I did my tank platoons and would have gladly traded an infantry squad for another good interpreter. An Arabic phrase the field guide does not contain, but which I had reason to use most often, was "Muterjiim Sayee," which means "Bad interpreter." It always defused rising tension when I was struggling to get my ideas across to a family whose house we were searching at three o'clock in the morning!

Although that useful phrase is missing, the guide is absolutely correct when it suggests that soldiers "Talk Arabic if you can to the people. No matter how badly you do it, they will like it." I can attest to this fact from constant personal experience. Just being able to convey normal greetings, and to introduce oneself according to local custom as "Abu Jack" (the father of Jack),[2] provided an enormous head start on building a number of relationships. As the guide states, "You should learn these [phrases] by heart" to succeed in the kind of warfare we are fighting today. It is far easier to defeat an insurgency with words than with machine guns. These

---

2. Arabs refer to men colloquially with reference to the name of their oldest son, in a manner similar to that of American street slang today ("Puff Daddy") or the naming convention that led to the common English last names "John's-son" and "Jack's-son." My photos of my own son Jack were such a great favorite among my Iraqi friends that I carried them wherever I went in a small pocket in front of my flak jacket for immediate access.

friendships my poor Arabic helped build ultimately bore fruit in actionable intelligence on enemy fighters in Khalidiyah.

The little guide is chock-full of the sort of practical wisdom that soldiers need to succeed today in what the Army's new Counterinsurgency Field Manual correctly calls "not just thinking man's warfare [but] the graduate level of war." Indeed, counterinsurgency turns many of the principles of conventional war upside down. In conventional warfare, finding one's enemy is comparatively easy, although he will use camouflage and deception in an attempt to hide from dangerous eyes. The key to victory is to mass firepower on his combat forces at the decisive point and time; thus in Desert Storm, I killed the tanks that didn't look like my own. In a counterinsurgency campaign, the enemy doesn't have the armor and firepower to compete in a fair fight, so he hides among civilians—in Mao's famous phrase, like a fish in the sea of the people. The hard part is not killing him, but finding him.

The key to success in a counterinsurgency campaign is providing enough security to the people that they feel empowered to reveal the identity of the killers who hide among them in plain sight. Once identified, insurgents are soft targets—but figuring out which two hundred or so of the sixty thousand people in your sector are trying to kill you is enormously difficult. They don't carry "I'm an Insurgent" identification cards. The local population will identify the insurgents to you, but only if they believe that you will be with them for the long haul to prevent reprisals. Building that kind of trust across cultures requires that the counterinsurgent deeply understand the local history and the people's culture, their customs, and their language. These are hard skills to master for an Army more accustomed to focusing on the basics of rifle marksmanship and artillery coordination. But to win this kind of war, an Army must move outside its comfort zone; the new Counterinsurgency Field Manual identifies "Learn and Adapt" as an imperative for success in counterinsurgency.

And this little manual can help. Much of the advice it contains is timeless, while some of it may be truer today than it was when it was written. "American success or failure in Iraq may well depend on whether the Iraqis (as the people are called) like American soldiers or not. It may not be quite that simple. But then again, it could." Defeating an insurgency depends upon providing security to the people, while unnecessary heavy-handedness loses hearts and minds—and gives insurgents the support they need to swim unreported among the sea of the people.

American soldiers now serving in Iraq, like those stationed in "the birthplace of mankind" in the 1940s, were assigned a historic task: "Years from now you'll be telling your children and maybe your grandchildren stories beginning, 'Now when I was in Baghdad——.'" The number of American soldiers able to begin war stories with those words is far greater today than it was at the conclusion of the Second World War, in which Iraq was far from the primary theater of war. There is no sign that it will stop increasing any time soon.

And yet despite the advice on nearly every page that sings to Marines and soldiers patrolling the streets of Baghdad and Ramadi as I write, there are also tips in the 1943 Short Guide that absolutely would not see the light of day in the politically correct world of today. None of the men serving there need to be told, "Don't make a pass at any Moslem women or there will be trouble." But the guide continues with more advice that caused my jaw to drop: "Anyway, it won't get you anywhere. Prostitutes do not walk the streets but live in special quarters of the cities." If service members today do need this guidance, I can absolutely guarantee that they won't get it from an official War Department publication!

Other things that wouldn't be printed today still need to be said. Perhaps none is more critical to everyday life than the warning that "You will have to carry your own supply of toilet paper." The Army supply system in Iraq has now caught up with that need, but care packages including this humble necessity were most welcome during the early days of America's occupation of Iraq.

Perhaps the greatest historical rhyme that resounds after reading this lovely little book is the underlying theme that marks every page and paragraph, every phrase in Arabic and in English. The guide is dedicated to the importance of the American mission in Iraq succeeding during the Second World War, for it was clearly recognized then that a free Iraq provided access to a ready flow of the oil that drove the American economy. The stakes are far higher today, with oil in shorter supply and the future of the entire Islamic world hanging in the balance. The guide simply informs soldiers and Marines, in words both challenging and poignant, that "If you can [win], it's going to be a better world for all of us."

As my Iraqi friends would say, "Inshallah."

LIEUTENANT COLONEL JOHN A. NAGL commands the 1st Battalion, 34th Armor at Fort Riley, Kansas. He is the author of *Learning to Eat Soup with a Knife: Counterinsurgency Lessons from Malaya and Vietnam* and was a contributing editor of U.S. Army Field Manual 3-24, *Counterinsurgency* (Marine Corps Warfighting Publication No. 3-33.5). Nagl served as the Operations Officer of Task Force 1-34 Armor in Khalidiyah, Iraq, from September 2003 through September 2004.

A SHORT GUIDE TO

IRAQ

WAR AND NAVY DEPARTMENTS
WASHINGTON, D. C.

Gift of Issuing office

CONTENTS

A SHORT GUIDE TO IRAQ

YOU HAVE been ordered to Iraq (i – RAHK) as part of the world-wide offensive to beat Hitler.

You will enter Iraq both as a soldier and as an individual, because on our side a man can be both a soldier and an individual. That is our strength—if we are smart enough to use it. It can be our weakness if we aren't. As a soldier your duties are laid out for you. As an individual, it is what you do on your own that counts—and it may count for a lot more than you think.

American success or failure in Iraq may well depend on whether the Iraqis (as the people are called) like American soldiers or not. It may not be quite that simple. But then again it could.

How To Beat Hitler.   Herr Hitler knows he's licked if the peoples united against him stand their ground. So it is pretty obvious what he and his propaganda machine are trying to do. They're trying to spread disunity and discontent among their opponents whenever and wherever they can.

———

So what's the answer? That ought to be pretty obvious, too. One of your big jobs is to prevent Hitler's agents from getting in their dirty work. The best way you can do this is by getting along with the Iraqis and making them your friends. And the best way to get along with any people is to understand them.

That is what this guide is for. To help you understand the people and the country so that you can do the best and quickest job of sending Hitler back where he came from.

And, secondly, so that you as a human being will get the most out of an experience few Americans have been lucky enough to have. Years from now you'll be telling your children and maybe your grandchildren stories beginning, "Now when I was in Baghdad ——."

WHAT is Iraq, anyhow? Well, it's a lot of things, old
and new. It is one of the oldest countries in the world—
and one of the youngest under its present government.
In Baghdad, the capital city, you will see street merchants selling exactly the same kind of pottery that their
ancestors sold at the time of the Arabian Nights. Not far
away you will see great dams and modern refineries equal
to the best you have seen in America. If you happen to be
sent to the oil fields, you will discover miracles of modern engineering construction side by side with primitive
refineries built 2,000 years ago and still in operation.

Iraq Is Hot! As a matter of fact, you may be so busy when
you reach Iraq that you won't see much of anything
for awhile. Probably you will feel Iraq first—and that
means heat. Blazing heat. And dust. In the daytime Iraq
can be one of the hottest spots in the world. If you happen to travel by train in the daytime, the leather seats
may get so hot that you'll have to stand up. Most work
is done between 6 a. m. and noon and perhaps an hour
or two in the early evening. And yet the nights of these
hot days are often uncomfortably cool.

Or maybe the first thing you notice will be the smells.
You have heard and read a lot about the "mysterious
East." You have seen moving pictures about the colorful
life of the desert and the bazaars. When you actually get

3

there you will look in vain for some of the things you have been led to expect. You will smell and feel a lot of things the movies didn't warn you about.

MEET THE PEOPLE

But don't get discouraged. Most Americans and Europeans who have gone to Iraq didn't like it at first. Might as well be frank about it. They thought it a harsh, hot, parched, dusty, and inhospitable land. But nearly all of these same people changed their minds after a few days or weeks, and largely on account of the Iraqi people they began to meet. So will you.

That tall man in the flowing robe you are going to see soon, with the whiskers and the long hair, is a first-class fighting man, highly skilled in guerilla warfare. Few fighters in any country, in fact, excell him in that kind of situation. If he is your friend, he can be a staunch and valuable ally. If he should happen to be your enemy— look out! Remember Lawrence of Arabia? Well, it was with men like these that he wrote history in the First World War.

But you will also find out quickly that the Iraqi is one of the most cheerful and friendly people in the world. Few people you have seen get so much fun out of work and everyday living. If you are willing to go just a little out of your way to understand him, everything will be o. k.

Differences? Of Course! Differences? Sure, there are differences. Differences of costume. Differences of food. Differences of manner and custom and religious beliefs. Different attitudes toward women. Differences galore.

But what of it? You aren't going to Iraq to change the Iraqis. Just the opposite. We are fighting this war to preserve the principle of "live and let live." Maybe that sounded like a lot of words to you at home. Now you have a chance to prove it to yourself and others. If you can, it's going to be a better world to live in for all of us.

Although relatively few Iraqis receive a formal education similar to yours, they are shrewd and intelligent and

tend to believe what they hear and see with their own ears and eyes. By what you do and how you act you can do a lot to win this war and the peace after it. Right now Iraq is threatened with invasion—as America is now. The Iraqis have some religious and tribal differences among themselves. Hitler has been trying to use these differences to his own ends. If you can win the trust and friendship of all the Iraqis you meet, you will do more than you may think possible to help bring them together in our common cause.

Needless to say, Hitler will also try to use the differences between ourselves and Iraqis to make trouble. But we have a weapon to beat that kind of thing. Plain common horse sense. Let's use it.

Hitler's game is to divide and conquer. Ours is to unite and win!

THE COUNTRY

First, let's have a look at the country. We can't very well talk about places and people until we know where we are.

In the center of this guide you will find a map of what is called the "Middle East." You will see by the map, Iraq lies south of Turkey; east of Syria and Palestine; north of Arabia; west of Iran (EE – RAHN) (Persia); and just touches the Persian Gulf at one corner. It is about the size of the State of Montana.

A Strategic Hot Spot. Iraq is thus a strategic part of the great "land bridge" between Europe and India—the road Hitler HOPES to use to join hands with his back-stabbing allies, the Japs. Also, the Persian Gulf is an important back door for us to get supplies to our Russian allies. And even more, Iraq has great military importance for its oil fields, with their pipelines to the Mediterranean Sea. Yes, Iraq is a hot spot in more ways than one.

Iraq was formerly called Mesopotamia. Its history goes back a tidy 5,000 years. By tradition the Garden of Eden was located in this region. Hence it is often called "the birthplace of mankind." It is certainly one of the oldest settled regions in the world. Here it was that the ancient cities of Babylon and Nineveh (NI – ne – ve) flourished in Bible times. You will very likely see their ruins, some of the great ruins of the world.

Before the First World War, Mesopotamia (as it was called then) was a part of Turkey. After the war the state of Iraq was set up as a British mandate, with an Arab chieftain, Feisal (FAY – sal), as king. In 1932 Iraq became an independent state—a "limited monarchy" of the English type, with an elected legislature. The present king is Feisal II, the grandson of the first king. Close relations have been maintained with the British, and the country is now guarded by British troops to prevent the Germans from gaining control.

★———————★

The Cities. Iraq has only a few cities. Baghdad, the largest, has a population of around 500,000, about like that of Minneapolis or Kansas City. Mosul (MO – sul) in the oil region has a population of over 100,000, Suq al – Shu yukh (SOOQ ash – shu – YOOKH) about the same, and Basrah (BAS – ra) on the Persian Gulf, the most important port, has about 70,000.

Most of Iraq is desert country. Not great sandy wastes like the Sahara in Africa, but flinty, harsh, monotonous desert, treeless but covered with a thin scrub vegetation very much like our Southwest region. The only water in this region comes from waterholes, and these are jealously guarded. Water is more valuable than anything else in the desert, and for the Iraqi, to waste water would be like throwing money away.

In contrast to the dry deserts are the great green valleys of the Tigris (TAI – gris) and Euphrates (yoo – FRAY – teez) Rivers. These two important rivers rise in the Kurdistan (KUR – di – stan) mountains of Turkey, north and west of Iraq. After flowing across the country in parallel channels, they join together and empty into the Persian Gulf through one mouth. In the valleys of these two rivers nine-tenths of the 3½ million people (about the population of Chicago) live.

At the northern end of these valleys is the important oil field of Kirkuk (kir – KOOK). The field was discovered in 1927 but it was not until 1935 that production began in earnest. Twin pipe-lines have been constructed to the ports of Tripoli in Syria and Haifa (HAI – fa) in Palestine, on the Mediterranean Sea. These fields and pipe-lines are among the richest prizes Hitler would like to grab, and they are heavily guarded. Guarding or defending them may be among your most important military duties, for this oil is the source of supply for the armies of the Middle East and India, and also feeds the Mediterranean fleet.

How the People Live. Nearly all farming in Iraq is dependent on irrigation, with water taken from the two great rivers. The most important crop is dates, which not only are the chief food of the people but also shipped to other countries. Grain, especially wheat, barley, rice, and millet is grown in large quantity. Also grown are cotton, sugar cane and legumes, with small quantities of citrus fruits.

Practically the only building material is dried mud, like the adobe used in the Southwestern U. S. A. It is admirably suited to the hot climate and you will find the inside of the flat-roofed Iraqi houses cool even in the noonday heat.

The Iraqi people are divided by occupation into the tradesmen in the cities, the farmers in the irrigated areas, and the nomads, who herd their sheep and camels on the desert, moving from place to place for fresh pastures.

The nomads and farmers cling to the native dress more than the city dwellers, who are often quite "westernized."

The nomads are divided into tribes headed by sheikhs (SHAYKH). These leaders are very powerful and should be shown great consideration. Townsmen, farmers, and nomads consider themselves as equals and should be treated as such.

THE MOSLEMS

THERE are a few Christians and Jews and other sects among the Iraqis, but by far the most people you will meet and see are Moslems. This means that they are followers of the religion founded by Mohammed. But you should not call it the Mohammedan religion, for the Moslems do not worship Mohammed as Christians worship Christ. They believe in one god, Allah, and that Mohammed was His prophet. The religion is called Islam and the people who believe in it are called Moslems.

The Moslem bible is known as the Koran and the Moslems worship in mosques (*mosks*). They are very devout in their religion and do not like to have "unbelievers" (to them you are an "unbeliever") come anywhere near their mosques. You can usually tell a mosque by its high tower. *Keep away from mosques.* Even though you may have visited mosques in Syria or Egypt, the mosques in Iraq must not be entered. If you try to enter one, you will be thrown out, probably with a severe beating. The Iraqi Moslems even resent unbelievers coming *close* to mosques. If you have blundered too near a mosque, get away in a hurry before trouble starts. The Moslem religion requires a man to pray five times a day. This is done by facing the holy city of Mecca and going through a series of prostrations. Don't stare at anyone who is praying, and above all do not make fun of him. Respect his religion as he will respect yours.

No Preaching.   This isn't preaching. You probably belong to a church at home, and you know how you would feel towards anyone who insulted or desecrated your church. The Moslems feel just the same way, perhaps even more strongly. In fact, their feeling about their religion is pretty much the same as ours toward our religion, although more intense. If anything, we should respect the Moslems the more for the intensity of their devotion.

There are four towns in Iraq which are particularly sacred to the Iraqi Moslems. These are Kerbela (ker – be – LAA), Nejef (NE – jef), Kadhiman (KAA – di – MAYN) (near Baghdad), and Samarra. Unless you are ordered to these towns, it is advisable to stay away from them.

It is a good idea in any foreign country to avoid any religious or political discussions. This is even truer in Iraq than most countries, because it happens that here the Moslems themselves are divided into two factions something like our division into Catholic and Protestant denominations—so don't put in your two cents worth when Iraqis argue about religion. There are also political differences in Iraq that have puzzled diplomats and statesmen. You won't help matters any by getting mixed up in them. Moreover, if you discuss foreign politics with them, you might be maneuvered into making statements that could be interpreted as criticisms of our Allies.

Your move is to stay out of political and religious arguments altogether. By getting into them you'll only help the Nazi propagandists who are trying to stir up trouble among the Iraqis.

IRAQI CUSTOMS AND MANNERS

MOST of the Iraqi customs and manners are religious in their origin. For example, there is the month of fasting each year called "Ramadan" (ra – ma – DAHN). This period is similar to the Lenten period in many of the Christian Churches. In 1942 Ramadan begins September 12th. In 1943 it will be about two weeks earlier. During this period the Moslems do not eat, drink, or smoke between sunrise and sunset. Avoid offering, or asking them for food, drink, or smokes at this time, except after sunset. All hesitations and refusals at this period should be accepted without any attempts at persuasion. Any drawing of blood, during this period, even if accidental, such as a scratch or a nosebleed, may have serious consequences. Remember that Moslem tempers are very short during this month as yours would be under similar circumstances.

The Moslem day of rest is Friday, and their stores are closed on that day. In Baghdad and the other large cities many shops are closed on Saturday, the Jewish day of rest, while Christian shops are closed on Sunday.

Moslems, Christians, and Jews all have a number of religious holidays. Some of these are solemn fasts like

Ramadan, others are colorful festivals. You will be wise to respect the observance of these holidays.

The "Evil Eye". Many of the Iraqis believe in the "evil eye". This is a good deal in their minds like putting a "hex" on a person is to people in parts of our country. If you stare at people, especially children, someone may think you are the possessor of an "evil eye", and are trying to put a curse on the person you are staring at. Some of the Iraqis think that the lens of a camera is an "evil eye", and you will make enemies by taking close-up snapshots and possibly wind up with a knife in your back. General views or street scenes will cause no trouble—except mosques. Don't try to photograph mosques.

Beggars are not numerous in Iraq. Those you will see live mainly in the cities and are mostly professionals, and it is not a good idea to give them money. If you do, the word will spread to all the beggars in the city that you are an easy mark. Of course, some of them may be deserving, and if you feel moved by their plight, give them a little something—but better be prepared to repeat.

Bargaining in the shops and bazzars is a great national pastime. You will have to bargain for almost everything you buy. The price first quoted is usually one-third to two-thirds higher than what you should pay. In bargaining the important thing is not to hurry. A little American horse trading will carry you a long way in this game.

BARGAINING TAKES TIME

Manners Are Important.   Moslems pay much attention to good manners.

Handshaking in Iraq is considered an important part of good manners. You will be greeted with a handshake on every occasion that you meet an Iraqi. His handshake is cordial and sincere. Return it in the same spirit.

But do not touch or handle an Iraqi in any other way. Do not wrestle with him in fun, and don't slap him on the back. Any such contact is offensive to his idea of good manners. Above all never strike an Iraqi.

Do your swearing in English. Avoid the native oaths—you will not know their exact meaning and they may get you into trouble. Don't under any circumstances call an Iraqi a "dog", a "devil", a "native", or a "heathen". These terms are all deadly insults to him.

They do not drink liquor or eat pork. So respect their feelings and do not drink in their presence. They do not like to see others drink and it offends them to see others drunk. Never give them pork to eat or offer it to them even in fun.

Pigs are "unclean" to Moslems. So are dogs. If you happen to have a mascot dog, be particularly careful to keep him away from mosques.

Moslems do not let other people see them naked. Do not urinate in their presence. They do it squatting and dislike to see other people do it standing up. These things may seem trivial, but they are important if you want to get along well with the Iraqis.

Moslem Women. Moslem women do not mingle freely with men. The greater part of their time they spend at home and in the company of their families. Never make advances to Moslem women or try to attract their attention in the streets or other public places. Do not loiter near them when they are shopping. If a woman has occasion to lift her veil while shopping, do not stare or smile at her. Look the other way. These rules are extremely important. The Moslems will immediately dislike you and there will be trouble if you do not treat women according to their standards and customs.

These rules apply both to the cities and towns and to the villages and the desert. The village and desert women go unveiled more often than the women in the cities and *seem* to have more freedom. But the rules are still strict. Any advance on your part will mean trouble and plenty of it. Even when speaking to Iraqi men, no mention should be made of their female relatives. The Iraqi them-

selves follow this custom and would resent anyone, especially a foreigner, not doing the same.

To repeat—don't make a pass at any Moslem woman or there will be trouble. Anyway, it won't get you anywhere. Prostitutes do not walk the streets but live in special quarters of the cities.

Iraqi Hospitality. If you are entertained in an Iraqi city home, you will probably find dishes and silverware and customs somewhat like our own. But do not eat too much of the first course of a meal. There is probably more coming.

In the country there will probably be no table, plates, or silverware. You will be expected to sit on the ground as your host does. Follow his example. Roll up your right sleeve and eat with the tips of your right fingers—even if you are a southpaw. It is considered rude to eat with your left hand. If your host tears off tid-bits and hands them to you, eat them. In the country there will probably be only one course. After the meal, water will be brought to wash your hands and a towel to wipe them.

In the desert the customs are much the same as in the country, except that there is less variety in the food. You may be offered only some bread and milk or soured milk, like buttermilk. These people are poor and are offering you the best they have. You must not refuse it—but do not take too much.

Coffee drinking is equally popular in the city, country, or desert. Even a shopkeeper may offer you a small glass of coffee. Do not refuse it or throw it away half-drunk, even if it does not taste like our American coffee. If you are offered a second cup, take it, and also a third. But it is customary to refuse a fourth.

These are some general hints about manners. But the main thing is the SPIRIT of politeness and courtesy. If you show this, the Iraqis will understand and forgive any lapses you may make through not knowing their customs. If you show that you really want to be friendly, you'll get along.

THE LANGUAGE

THE native language of Iraq is Arabic. You will not need to know many words to get along. A few simple words will go a long way. Learn a few words and

THE FOURTH IS OUT!

phrases—you will find a helpful list at the end of this guide—and talk to the Iraqis in their own language. They will like it even if your pronunciation is not the same as theirs. They will be especially pleased when you use their polite salutations even if you do not know any other words. When you hear one of them speak English— no matter how badly—you will understand the pleasure they feel when you speak to them in their language.

Many Iraqis speak a few words or at least understand English, especially those in the larger stores in the cities and others in the oil regions which were developed by the British. Occasionally among the wealthier classes French, Turkish, and sometimes German are spoken. In most of the Baghdad bazaars, Persian is understood. From Mosul north both Turkish and Kurdish are heard commonly.

CLIMATE AND HEALTH—SANITARY CONDITIONS

IRAQ is a hot country. This means: keep your headgear on when you are in the summer sun. In this kind of a climate it is very easy to let yourself be burned and think nothing of it. But next day you are likely to wake up with black blisters and possible fever. The headgear issued to you will be sufficient to protect you. But whatever you wear, be sure that it shades the back of your neck as well as the top of your head. If you expose the back of your

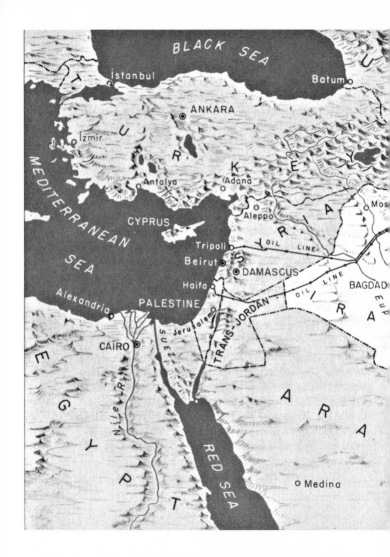

neck you are inviting sunstroke. Don't, under any circumstances, take a sun bath.

In the desert, be prepared for extremes of temperature. The days are usually very hot. The nights can be uncomfortably cool.

Boil your drinking water or see that it is properly chlorinated. You will find that conditions of life in Iraq do not allow the degree of sanitation or cleanliness that we know.

Avoid eating unwashed vegetables and fruits. They may be contaminated by human excrement. Wash raw fruits and vegetables in water or alcohol or peel them before eating them, because the skins may have become contaminated by flies or by human contact. Avoid leafy vegetables altogether. Keep all food away from flies.

Diseases: Malaria and typhoid are two very serious fevers. You should guard against them in every possible way. Malaria is carried by a particular kind of mosquito which breeds in marshy areas, uncovered wells and cisterns and in shallow water pools. If at all possible, stay away from areas in which malaria is common. When you

can't do this, sleep under nets and keep your arms and legs covered, especially at dusk.

Typhoid is contracted from unboiled water and from raw foods which have not been properly cleaned or peeled. Once again, avoid them.

Sandflies, which are smaller than mosquitos and which can get through an ordinary mosquito net, carry a slight three-day fever which is not serious but is very weakening. It is known as sandfly fever. Sandflies are most prevalent in midsummer. Coating yourself with a light oil will give you some protection from them.

You should be very careful about bugs and lice, which are common. Give yourself a frequent once-over for them. Scabies is a skin infection, produced by a parasite which feeds on the skin. It is extremely annoying and difficult to get rid of. However, it can be cured by sulphur ointment.

Intestinal diseases, such as dysentery and tapeworm, are very common in Iraq. These can be avoided, or at least made less severe, by extreme care in the water you drink and the food you eat.

Trachoma, a very common disease of the eye, can be picked up almost everywhere, even from shaking hands with someone and then touching your eyes. *Don't rub or touch your eyes.*

Toilets such as those in America are very scarce. You will have to get used to relieving yourself outdoors at any convenient spot. Be sure to get well off the main streets and well away from mosques, and out of sight as much as possible. You will have to carry your own supply of toilet paper.

There is a good deal of venereal disease around, so don't take chances.

CURRENCY, WEIGHTS, MEASURES, ETC.

Iraqi Currency. The rate of exchange of Iraqi money to United States currency may vary a little from time to time, so that the table below can give only approximate ratios. The basis of Iraqi money is the "dinar" (DEE – NAHR) which is roughly worth $4.00 in United States money. Each dinar is further divided into 1,000 "fils" (fils or FI – lis). The dinar is a paper note or bill; the fils pieces are coin. The approximate value of the various denominations of Iraqi money are given below.

TABLE OF IRAQ CURRENCY

Paper Money

Iraq Value	American Dollars
100 Dinars	$402.00
10 Dinars	40.20
5 Dinars	20.10
1 Dinar	4.02
½ Dinar (500 fils)	2.01
¼ Dinar (250 fils)	1.00

Silver Coins

200 fils	.80
50 fils	.20
20 fils	.08

Nickel Coins

10 fils	.04
4 fils	.016

Bronze Coins

2 fils	.008
1 fils	.004

An easy way to remember the values of the various fils pieces is to think of each fils as being worth just a little less than ½ cent in U. S. money.

★——————————★

The Moslem Calendar.   The Moslem calendar is used in Iraq. The main thing to know about the Moslem calendar is that it is lunar, or based on the moon. Each of the 12 months has only 28 days. This means that the Moslem year is a little shorter than our year, so that a special date, such as the fast of Ramadan, will occur a little earlier each year.

Time.   There are two ways of telling time in Iraq. The official system is the "European system." That is, a 24-hour clock, beginning at midnight, instead of a 12-hour clock. So in railway timetables you may see that a train is scheduled to arrive at 14 o'clock. That means at 2 p. m. as we reckon time. Or at 23 o'clock, which is 11 p. m. to us. 24 o'clock is midnight. However, most of the country goes on the same 12-hour system used in America.

Weights and Measures.   The metric system is used for all official measurements of distance and area in Iraq. The unit of length in the metric system is the "meter," which is 39.37 inches, or a little more than our yard. The unit of road distance is the "kilometer," which is 1,000 meters or ⅝ (a little over one-half) of one of our miles.

The metric unit of square measure is the "hectare" (*HECK-tayr*), which consists of 10,000 square meters, or about 2½ of our acres. An Iraqi unit of square measure is the dunam (*DU-nam*) or "misharah (*mi-SHAH-ra*), which equals 2,500 square meters or a little less than 3,000 square yards.

The unit of weight in the metric system is the "kilogram," which equals 2.2 pounds in our system.

Liquids in the metric system are measured by the "liter." A liter is a little more than one of our quarts.

SOME IMPORTANT DO'S AND DON'TS

Keep away from mosques.

Smoke or spit somewhere else—never in front of a mosque.

If you come near a mosque, keep moving (away) and don't loiter.

Keep silent when the Moslems are praying (which they do five times a day) and don't stare.

Discuss something else—*NEVER* religion or politics or women—with Moslems.

Remember the fear of the "evil eye." Don't stare at anyone. Don't point your camera in anyone's face.

Avoid offering opinions on internal politics.

Shake hands with the Iraqi; otherwise don't touch them or slap them on the back.

Remember that the Iraqi are a very modest people and avoid any exposure of the body in their presence.

Keep out of the sun whenever you can. When you can't, keep your head and neck covered.

Start eating only after your host has begun.

Eat with your right hand—never with your left, even if you are a southpaw.

Always tear bread with your fingers—never cut it.

Bread to the Moslems is holy. Don't throw scraps of it about or let it fall on the ground.

In the city eat only part of the first course. There may be more coming.

In the country leave some food in the bowl—what you leave goes to the women and children.

Don't offer Moslems food containing pork, bacon, or lard, or cooked in pork products. All such food is religiously "unclean" to them.

Don't eat pork or pork products in front of Moslems.

Be pleasant if Moslems refuse to eat meat you offer.

Don't offer Moslems alcoholic drinks. Drink liquor somewhere else—never in the presence of Moslems.

MEAL TIME TIPS FOR SOUTHPAWS

Knock before entering a private house. If a woman answers, wait until she has had time to retire.

Always respect the Moslem women. Don't stare at them. Don't smile at them. Don't talk to them or follow them. If you do any of these things, it means trouble for you and your unit.

In a house or tent, follow the rule of your host. If he takes off his shoes on entering, do the same.

If you are required to sit on the floor in an Iraqi house or tent, cross your legs while doing so.

When visiting, don't overstay your welcome. The third glass of tea or coffee is the signal to leave unless you are quartered there.

If you should see grown men walking hand in hand, ignore it. They are not "queer."

Be kind and considerate to servants. The Iraqis consider all people equals.

Avoid any expression of race prejudice. The people draw very little color line.

Talk Arabic if you can to the people. No matter how badly you do it, they will like it.

Shake hands on meeting and leaving.

On meeting an Iraqi, be sure to inquire after his health.

If you wish to give someone a present, make it sweets or cigarettes.

If you are stationed in the country, it is a good idea to take sweets and cigarettes with you when you visit an Iraqi's home.

Show respect toward all older persons. If serving food, the eldest person should be served first.

Be polite. Good manners are important to the Iraqis. Be hospitable.

Bargain on prices. Don't let shopkeepers or merchants overcharge you; but be polite.

Be generous with your cigarettes.

Above all, use common sense on all occasions. And remember that every American soldier is an unofficial ambassador of good will.

THESE are pronunciation hints to help you in listening to the Arabic language records which have been supplied to your troop unit. They will also help you with the pronunciation of additional words and phrases given in the vocabulary below, which are not included in the records.

Arabic is spoken over a great area in North Africa and the Near East. There are some differences between regions, both in pronunciation and the use of words. The dialect you are going to hear on this set of records is the Baghdad variety and you will be understood all over Iraq, except in the extreme north, and in most of Trans-Jordania. If you should go on to other regions, you will be given further information at that time. Don't worry about that now.

There is nothing very difficult about Arabic—except that you won't be able to read Arabic signs and newspapers you will see. That is because they use a different alphabet from ours. Therefore, the instructions and vocabulary below are not based on the written Arabic language, but are a simplified system of representing the language as it *sounds*. This system contains letters for all the sounds you *must* make to be understood. It does *not* contain letters for some of the sounds you will hear, but it will give you enough to get by on, both listening and speaking.

Here are a few simple rules to help you:

1. *Accents.* You know what the accented syllable of a word is, of course. It is the syllable which is spoken louder than the other syllables in the same word. We will show accented (loud) syllables in capital letters and unaccented syllables in small letters.

2. *Vowels.* These are the kinds of sounds we represent in English by *a, e, i, o, u, ah, ay, ei, oi, au, ow,* etc. Just follow the key below and you will have no trouble.

a or A	equals	The *a* in *pat* or the *o* in *pot*. There is no fixed rule. You'll just have to listen and learn. (Example: *tif-HAM-nee* meaning "do you understand me"?)
AA	equals	The *a* in *bath*—that is, not the "broad *a*"—but stretch (lengthen) it. (Example: *THLAA-tha* meaning "three".)
AH	equals	The *a* in *father*—that is, the "broad *a*",—but stretch it. (Example: *WAH-hid* meaning "one".)
AI	equals	The *ai* in *aisle*—but stretch it. (Example: *MAI* meaning "water".)
AU	equals	The *ow* in *now*—but stretch it. Example: *AU-wal* meaning "first".)
AY	equals	The *ay* in *day*—but stretch it. (Example: *WAYN* meaning "where".)
e or E	equals	The *e* in *pet*. (Example: *tel* meaning "hill".)
ee or EE	equals	The *ee* in *feet*—but stretch it. (Example: *a-REED* meaning "I want".)
i or I	equals	The *i* in *pit*. (Example: *SIT-te* meaning "six".)

o or O	equals	The *o* in *go*—but stretch it. (Example: *YOM* meaning "day".)
OO	equals	The *oo* in *boot*—but stretch it. (Example: *ar-JOOK* meaning "please".)
u or U	equals	The *u* in *put*. (Example: *NUS* meaning "half".)
uh or UH	equals	The *u* in *but*. (Example: *CHUHZ-ma* meaning 'boots'.)

3. *Consonants.* The consonants are all the sounds that are not vowels. Pronounce them just as you know them in English. *All* consonants should be pronounced. Never "slight" them. Here are some special consonant sounds to learn.

h	small *h* is always pronounced with the *h* sound except after small *u*. Listen carefully to the *h* sound on the records.
kh	is pronounced as when clearing your throat when you have to spit. Listen carefully for it on the records.
gh	is pronounced like *kh* except that you put "voice" into it. That is, a sound very much as when you gargle.
sh	is like the *sh* in *show*.
th	is like the *th* in *thin*.
dh	is like the *th* in *then*.
ch	is like the *ch* in *church*.
q	is like a very far back *k*, that is, it is swallowed. Listen carefully for it on the records.
(')	is to be pronounced like a slight cough. Listen carefully for it on the records. Whenever it

is indicated, pronounce it clearly, but do not pronounce it even accidentally when it is not indicated, or you will be misunderstood.

s   is always pronounced like the *s* in *kiss*.

LIST OF MOST USEFUL WORDS AND PHRASES

HERE is a list of the most useful words and phrases you will need in Arabic. *You should learn these by heart.* They are the words and phrases included on the Arabic language records, and appear here in the order they occur on the records.

Greetings and General Phrases

English—*Simplified Arabic Spelling*

good day—*saBAHh il-KHAYR*

good evening—*ma-sal KHAYR*

sir—*BAYG*

madam—*KHAH-TOON* (but if the lady is a Moslem)—*KHAH-nim*

miss—*BNAY-ye*

please (to a man)—*ar-JOOK* or *min-FADH-lak*

please (to a woman) — *ar-JOOCH* or *min-FADH-lich*

please (to more than one person)—*ar-JOO-kum* or *min-Jadh-IL-kum*

pardon me—*il-'A-Ju*

excuse me (to a man)—*u'-DHUR-nee*

excuse me (to a woman)—*u'-dhur-EE-nee*

excuse me (to more than one person)—*u'-dhur-OO-nee*

thank you (to a man)—*ash-KU-rak*

Thank you (to a woman)—*ash-KU-rich*

Thank you (to more than one person)—*ash-KUR-kum*

Yes—*NA-'am*

No—*la'*

Do you understand me—*tif-HAM-nee*

I don't understand—*MA-da-AF-ham*

Please speak slowly—*ar-JOOK, Eh-chee ya-WAHSH*

Location

Where (is)—*WAYN*
   a restaurant—*il-MAT-'am*
Where is a restaurant—*WAYN il-MAT-'am*
   a hotel—*il-OO-TAYL*
Where is a hotel—*WAYN il-OO-TAYL*
   the railroad station—*il ma-HAT-ta*

Where is the R. R. station—*WAYN il-ma-HAT-ta*
   a toilet—*il-A-dab*
Where is a toilet—*WAYN il-A-dab*

Directions

Turn right—*DOOR YIM-ne*
Turn left—*DOOR YIS-re*
Straight ahead—*GU-bal*

Please point—*ar-JOOK, ra-WEE-nee*

If you are driving and ask the distance to another town, it will be given you in kilometers as often as miles.

Kilometers—*KEE-lo-met-RAHT*   Miles—*MEEL*

One kilometer equals ⅝ of a mile. You need to know the numbers.

Numbers

One—*WAH-hid*
Two—*THNAYN*
Three—*THLAA-tha*

Four—*AR-ba-'a*
Five—*KHAM-sa*

When you use the numbers with other words, you just say the number and add the other word

One kilometer—*WAH-hid KEE-lo-ME-tir*

But two kilometers you say "couple of kilometers" all in one word.

Two kilometers—*KEE-lo-met-RAYN*

Three kilometers—*THLAA-tha KEE-lo-ME-tir*

Six—*SIT-te*

Seven—*SAB-'a*

Eight—*THMAA-nee-a*

Nine—*TIS-'a*

Ten—*'ASH-re*

Eleven—*DA-'ash*

Twelve—*THNA-'ash*

Thirteen—*thla-TA'SH*

Fourteen—*ar-ba'-TA'SH*

Fifteen—*khu-mus-TA'SH*

Sixteen—*sit-TA'SH*

Seventeen—*sba-TA'SH*

Eighteen—*thmun-TA'SH*

Nineteen—*tsa-TA'SH*

Twenty—*'ish-REEN*

For "twenty-one", "thirty-two" and so forth, you put the number before the words for "twenty" and "thirty," just as we sometimes say "one and twenty", thus:

Twenty-one — *WAH-hid u-'ish REEN*

Thirty—*THLAA-THEEN*

Thirty - two — *THNAYN u - THLAA-THEEN*

Forty—*ar-ba-'EEN*

Fifty—*kham-SEEN*

One hundred—*MEE-YE*

But for 200 you would say "couple of hundreds", all in one word—

Two hundred—*MEE-TAYN*

For 250 you say "couple of hundreds and fifty"—

250 — *MEE-TAYN u-kham-SEEN*

For 255 you say "couple of hundreds, five and fifty"—

255 — *MEE-TAYN u-kham-sa u-kham-SEEN*

But for 555 you would say "five hundred and five and fifty"—

555—*klam-is MEE-ye u-kham-sa u-kham-SEEN*

1,000 — *A-lif*

Designation

What is—*SHI-nu*
This—*HAA-dha*
What's this—*SHI-nu HAA-dha*
I want—*a-REED*
   cigarettes—*ji-GAA-yir*

I want cigarettes—*a-REED ji-GAA-yir*
   to eat—*AH-kul*
I want to eat—*a-REED AH-kul*

Foods

Bread—*KHU-buz*
Fruit—*MAY-we*
Water—*MAI*
Eggs—*BAY-uhdh*
Steak (but only in cities)—
   STAYK
Meat—*LA-ham*
Potatoes—*pu-TAY-ta*
Rice—*TIM-man*
Beans (navy)—*fa-sul-EE-a*
Beans (horse)—*BAA-GIL-la*
Fish—*SI-mach*
Salad—*za-LAH-ta*

Milk—*ha-LEEB*
Beer—*BEE-ra*
A glass of beer—*GLAHS BEE-ra*
A cup of coffee—*fin-JAHN GAh-wa*
To find out how much things cost, you say:
How much—*shgad*
   costs—*i-KAL-lif*
   this—*HAA-dha*
How much does this cost?—
   shgad i-KAL-lif HAA-dha

Money

fils—*FI-lis*
Two fils ("couple of fils")—
   fil-SAYN
Four fils—*AR-ba-'a FLOOS*
Fifty fils—*kham-SEEN FI-lis*
   or—*WAH-hid DIR-ham*
Two hundred fils—*MEE-TAYN FI-lis*
   or—*WAH-hid ree-ALL*

Dinar—*DEE-NAHR*
Two Dinars—*DEE-NAA-RAYN*
Four Dinars—*AR-ba-'a DEE-NAHR*

Time

What time is it—*SAA-'a BAYSH*

Quarter past five—*KHAM-sa u-RU-bu'*

Half past six—*SIT-a u-NUS*

Twenty past seven—*sab-'a u THI-lith*

Twenty of eight—*THMAA-nee-a IL-la THIL-ith*

"Except a quarter"—*IL-la RU-bu'*

Quarter of two—*thin-TAYN IL-la RU-bu'*

Ten minutes to three—*THLAA-tha IL-la 'ASH-ra*

At what time—*SAA-'a BAYSH* the movie—*is-SEE-na-ma* starts—*tib-TI-dee*

At what time does the movie start?—*SAA-'a BAYSH tib-TI-dee is-SEE-na-ma*

The train—*il-qit-TAHR* leaves—*YIM-shee*

At what time does the train leave?—*SAA-'a BAYSH YIM-shee il-qit-TAHR*

Today—*il-YOM* or—*hal-YOM*

Tomorrow—*BAA-chir*

Days of the week:

Sunday—*il-'A-had*

Monday—*il-ith-NAYN*

Tuesday—*ith-tha-la-THAA*

Wednesday—*il-ar-ba-'AH*

Thursday—*il-ḳha-MEES*

Friday—*il-JUM-'a*

Saturday—*is-SE-bit*

Useful phrases:

What is your name (to a man)—*SHIS-mak*

What is your name (to a woman)—*SHIS-mich*

My name is —— *IS-mee* ————

How do you say —— in Arabic?—*SHLON TGOOL —— bil-'A-ra-bee*

Good-bye (by person leaving)—*FEE a-MAAN il-LAAh*

Good-bye (by person replying)—*ma-'as-sa-LAA-ma*

ADDITIONAL WORDS AND PHRASES

[English—*Arabic*]

Surroundings—Natural Objects

bank (of river)—*JUR-uf*
darkness—*dha-LAAM*
daytime (light)—*na-HAAR*
desert—*sah-RAH'* or *CHOL*
field—*SAA-ha*
fire—*NAAR*
grass—*ha-SHEESH*
the ground—*GAA'*
hill—*tel*
ice—*THE-lij*
lake—*bu-HAI-ra*
the moon—*il-GU-mar*

mountain—*JI-bal*
the ocean (sea)—*BA-har*
rain—*MU-tar*
river—*NA-har* or *shuht*
snow—*WA-fur*
spring (water-hole, etc.)—*'AYN*
the stars—*in-nu-JOOM*
stream—*NA-har*
the sun—*ish SHA-mis*
swamp—*mus-TAN-qa'*
wind—*REEh* or *HA-wa*

Time

day—*YOM*
day after tomorrow—*'U-gub BAH-chir*
day before yesterday—*AU-wal BAHR-ha*
evening—*ma-SAA'*
month—*SHA-har*
morning—*SU-BAh*
night—*LAYL*
week—*is-BOO'*
year—*SA-na*
yesterday—*il-BAHR-ha*
January—*KAA-NOON THAA-nee*

February—*shu-BAHT*
March—*AH-DHAHR* or *MAHRT*
April—*NEE-SAAN*
May—*MAIS* or *ay-YAHR*
June—*ho-zay-RAHN*
July—*tam-MOOZ*
August—*AAB*
September—*AY-LOOL*
October—*tish-REEN AU-wal*
November—*tish-REEN THAA-nee*
December—*KAA-NOON AU-wal*

Relationships

boy—*WA-lad*
brother—*uhkh*
child—*TU-fil*
daughter—*BI-nit*
father—*ab*

man—*RA-jul* or *rij-JAAL*
mother—*um*
sister—*U-khut*
son—*I-bin*
woman—*MA-ra*

Human Body

arms—*EE-DAYN*
back—*DHA-har*
eye—*'AYN*
finger—*IS-ba'*
foot—*QA-dam*
hair—*SHA-'ar*

hand—*FED*
head—*RAHS*
leg—*RI-jil*
mouth—*HA-lig*
nose—*KHA-shim*
teeth—*SNOON*

House and Furniture

bed—*FRAHSH*
blanket—*bat-TAH-NEE-ya*
 or *blanket*
chair—*SKAM-lee*
door—*BAAB*
drinking water—*MAI SHU-rub*
house—*BAYT*

stairs—*da-RAJ*
stove (cooking place)—*MO-gad*
table—*MAYZ*
wall—*HAH-yit*
water for washing—*MAI GHA-*
 sil
window—*shib-BAACH*

Food and Drink—Tobacco

butter—*ZI-bid*
cigars—*si-GAHR*
food—*A-kil*
pipe—*PEEP*
salt—*MI-lih*

sugar—*SHA-kar*
tea—*CHAI*
tobacco—*TI-tin*
wine—*sha-RAHB*

★———————★

Surroundings

bridge—*JI-sir*
mosque—*JAH-mi'*
church—*ka-NEE-sa*
mosque (small)—*MAS-jid*
city—*BAL-da*
path (trail, pass)—*ta-REEQ*
post-office—*POS-ta*
road—*ta-REEQ*
shop (store)—*duk-KAHN* or
  MAKH-zan or *ma-GHAA-za*
  (dept. store)

street—*SHAA-ri'*
town—*BA-lad*
village—*QAR-ya*
well—*BEER*
police-post—*MAKH-far SHUR-*
  ta

Animals

animal—*hai-WAHN*
bird—*TAYR*
camel—*JI-mal*
chicken (hen)—*di-JAH-ja*
cow—*HAl-sha*
dog—*CHE-lib*
donkey (burrow, jackass)—
  ZMAHL
goat—*SA-khal, 'AN-za* (female
  goat)

horse—*ha-SAHN*
mouse—*FAHR*
mule—*BA-ghal*
pig—*khan-ZEER*
rabbit—*AR-nab*
rat—*JRAY-dee*
sheep—*kha-ROOF*
snake—*HAl-ya*

Trades and Occupations

baker—*khuhb-BAHZ*
barber—*im-ZAY-yin*
blacksmith—*had-DAHD*
butcher—*gas-SAHB*

cook—*tab-BAHKH*
farmer—*fal-LAAh*
shoemaker—*rag-GAH'*
tailor—*khai-YAHT*

Numbers

sixty—*sit-TEEN*
seventy—*sab-'EEN*
eighty—*THMAA-NEEN*
ninety—*tis-'EEN*
first—*AU-wal*
second—*THAA-nee*
third—*THAA-lith*
fourth—*RAH-bi'*

fifth—*KHAH-mis*
sixth—*SAA-dis*
seventh—*SAA-bi'*
eighth—*THAA-min*
ninth—*TAA-si'*
tenth—*'AH-shir*
eleventh—*it-DA-'ash*
twelfth—*il-THNA-'ash*

Clothing

belt—*ha-ZAHM*
boots—*CHUHZ-ma*
coat—*PAHL-to* (overcoat) or *CHA-KET* (suitcoat)
gloves—*chi-FOOF*
hat—*SHAF-ḳa*
necktie—*BAYIM-BAHGH*

shirt—*THOB*
shoes—*QUN-da-ra*, (pl.) *qa-NAH-dir*
socks—*JOO-RAH-BAHT*
trousers—*pan-TROON*
undershirt—*fa-NAY-la*

Adjectives

good—*ZAYN*
bad—*MOO-ZAYN*
big—*chi-BEER*
small—*zi-GHAI-yir*
sick—*waj-'AHN*
well—*ZAYN*
lame—*A'-raj*
hungry—*JOO-'AHN*
thirsty—*'at-SHAHN*
black—*AS-wad*
white—*AB-yad*
red—*Ah-mar*
blue—*AZ-rag*

green—*AKH-dhar*
yellow—*UHS-far*
high—*'AH-lee*
low—*NAH-see*
cold—*BAA-rid* (of things) or *bar-DAHN* (of persons)
hot—*HAHR*
wet—*im-BAL-lal*
dry—*NAH-shif* or *YAH-bis*
expensive—*GHAH-lee*
cheap—*ra-KHEES*
empty—*FAH-righ*
full—*mat-ROOS* or *mal-YAAN*

Pronouns, etc.

1—*AA-nee* or *A-na*

we—*Ah-na*

you—*IN-ta* (masc. sg.); *IN-ti* (fem. sg.) *IN-tu* (pl.)

he—*HOO-wa*

she—*HEE-ya*

they—*HUM-ma* (masc.) *HIN-na* (fem.)

this—*HAA-dha* (masc.) *HAA-dhee* (fem.)

my—*MAA-lee*

these *DHO-le*

that — *DHAHK* (m a s c.) (*DHEECH* (fem.)

those—*DHO-LAHK* (masc. and fem.)

who—*MI-nu*

what—*SHI-nu*

how many—*CHUHM WAH-hid*

how far—*shgad bi-'EED*

anyone—*AI WAH-hid*

Prepositions

for—*I-la*

from—*min*

in—*bi*

of—*min*

on—*'A-la*

to—*I-la*

up to—*I-la* or *li-HAD*

with—*WEE-ye*

Adverbs

above—*FOG*

again—*MAR-ra THAH-nee-a*

behind—*WA-ra*

beside—*'A-la SAF-ha*

below—*JAU-wa*

far—*bi-'EED*

here—*he-NAH*

in front—*gid-DAHM*

less—*a-QAL*

more—*ZAA-yid*

near—*qa-REEB*

on that side—(see "there")

on this side—(see "here")

there—*he-NAHK*

very—*HWAI-yir*

Conjunctions

and—*wa* or *u*

but—*LAA-kin*

if—*I-dha*

or—*AU*

that—*in*

What date is today?—*hal-YOM shgad*

Today is the fifth of June—*hal-YOM KHAM-sa ho-zay-RAHN*

What day of the week?—*hal-YOM SHI-nu*

Today is Tuesday, etc.—*hal-YOM ith-tha-la-THAA*

Come here—*ta-'AAL hi-NAA*

Come quickly—*ta-'AAL bil-'A-jal*

Go quickly—*ROOh bil-'A-jal*

Who are you?—*MI-nu In-ta*

What do you want?—*shit-REED*

Bring some drinking water—*JEEB MAI li-SHU-rub*

Bring some food—*JEEB SHWAY-yat A-kil*

How far is the camp?—*shgad bi-'EED il-ma-'AS-kar*

How far is the water?—*shgad bi-'EED il-MAI*

Whose house is this?—*BAYT man HAA-dha*

☆ U S GOVERNMENT PRINTING OFFICE : 1943 - O - 508795